INVESTING IN THE STOCK MARKET

A Guide to Find and Invest in Equities
&
Ensure Building of Long Term Wealth

By Marc Possley

Introduction:

My intent in writing this book was to describe an
uncomplicated investment plan for individuals. This
plan is focused on direct purchase of equities and
ETFs (Exchange Traded Funds) and is intended to be
a long-term buy and hold program for accumulation
of wealth for retirement purposes.

Table of Contents:

Foreword

If you want to "Hit it out of the park" with stocks, this book is not for you.

If you want to build wealth and are willing to make small sacrifices, both in time and money, this book may be for you. This is intended to be especially helpful for the beginner. If you feel that you would like to understand how to take control of your own investments and minimize fees, please read on.

First you must dismiss the concept of speculating on stocks. This is a form of gambling and has nothing to do with responsible investing. Secondly, forget the technical methods which employ exotic charting methods to predict stock behavior. Some people make money using technical highly advanced methods, but many lose. The same can be said of patrons of a casino. Next, learn how to evaluate a stock. There is a lot of power in spending even a short time (5-10 minutes) to look at a stock and categorize it as having growth and/or value. Finally, once you have selected a stock, you need to have a buying strategy for the stock. (When and how do you buy it? At what price?).

Within this book, the intention is to present a foundation for investing in stocks. The ideas and strategies laid out in this book were not invented by the author. It is a summation of readily available information from experience. This includes conservative investment information by highly regarded authors. If you read only one book on investing, make it *The Intelligent Investor* by Benjamin Graham. The reader is urged to outline the book

as you read it. This outline could be an especially helpful file to keep as a shortcut on your computer desktop.

This book assumes that the reader knows how to use the on-line broker's software. If this is not the case, please be sure to become familiar with the software of the specific broker you plan to use. Most brokers will permit opening of an account prior to making deposits. This will permit you to review the instructive material provided by the broker.

Strategies

This book is for the purpose of building wealth through investment, as opposed to attempting to achieve the same goal through speculation. The term "investing" means simply that we are lowering our risk of loss by using tools to buy very solid stocks of companies that are well run. Our presumption is that we will get a reasonable reward over time not only from the increase in stock price but also from dividends.

Below are the recommended strategies for individuals to consider for their investment program.

Strategy #1:
Manage your own investment portfolio

Why do we want to do this ourselves rather than simply turn our money over to a wealth manager and let him/her do all the work? The three best reasons are:

1. We avoid paying a wealth manager 1% to 2% of our wealth each year to manage our money. This payment is made whether your account has an increase in a given year (and there will be down years.)

2. It is very hard to know which wealth manager will be working for your best interest, rather than for his own.

3. Wealth managers almost invariably put their client's money into funds which are managed at the fund level, not by the wealth manager. These funds have added daily transaction costs which are not reported in the "Total Cost" of the fund. Such costs can be significant (1/2 to 1% is common and many funds are even more expensive.)

Strategy #2:
Do not invest funds that you may need in the future

Using the fund as a piggy bank not only defeats your main goal of investing for the long haul (i.e. retirement), but withdrawal when the need arises often is at a disadvantageous time from an investment growth viewpoint.

If you start with a lump sum, make sure you have enough set aside to meet your anticipated needs for such items as home repairs, car expenses, etc. Plus, include at least 3-6 months living expenses depending on how secure you feel about your income.
If you start with a smaller sum plus a monthly contribution, make sure the monthly contribution is something you can afford to remove from your personal cash flow. For instance, you may want to consider your monthly take-home pay, and then set aside 5% of that for a monthly contribution. If you are lucky enough to get significant income increases

in the future, you would profit greatly by increasing your monthly contribution by 10-25% of the take-home pay which resulted from the increase.

Strategy #3:
Never buy a stock based on a tip, a hunch, or advice from a talking head

If you develop informal discussion groups and someone whom you know to be knowledgeable recommends a stock, ask him why. It may be a good recommendation, but it should be based on research – not because of a "tip."

There are people and firms who track the stock performance and make recommendations based on what are called "Technical Indicators." Most of these use various charting techniques of the past performance to predict future performance. These technical strategies work some of the time. When losses do occur, and they will, they are very hard to recover from. A lot of small investors claim they do quite well by these methods, but this is difficult and risky. If you are new to investing, you would be well advised to stay away from these risky methods.

Strategy #4:
Do your own research on stocks. (See discussion on research in Appendix 1.)

This sounds like a daunting task, but in fact it is quite easy to do some basic research. Appendix I has a discussion of a method for basic research. If you really don't want to do research, you still have a chance for a good portfolio if you buy, for example, only S&P 4 and 5 star rated stocks. These are very good stocks for the long term. There are, however, some things you can do to improve your selection by researching within this excellent group of stocks. As a few examples: You may glance at the fundamentals and see that there are negative earnings trends. Or you may look at the Corporate Debt and see that it is disturbingly high with significant short-term debt which is expensive. We will discuss these types of considerations in the Appendix.

Strategy #5:
Buy highly rated stocks which have value and growth potential.

There are many firms which will provide ratings of any stocks you may be interested in. These rating firms may use different measurements of a company's worth. Some firms use technical indicators while other firms use Value or Growth Potential. In actual practice, the rating firms use various combinations of "worth" to rate the stocks. This strategy does not favor technical indicators (charting.)

I personally use Standard and Poors (S&P), Reuters, and Morningstar ratings. I like S&P the best because it looks at value and growth and this data is also very easy to access through Scottrade which happens to be the firm I use for on-line investing. Other rating systems and other on-line brokers are equally satisfactory for this purpose.

Strategy #6:
Diversify

Diversification simply means that you spread out your investment dollars over several different stocks and/or sectors. The theory is that you lower your risk through diversification because no single stock or sector can impact your portfolio any more than its allocation.

Articles have been written by experts who suggest you are sufficiently diversified with as little as eight different equities. Other articles suggest twenty or so. While the larger number may be better, this is often driven by how much money you can devote to your investment plan.

If you are blessed with a large amount of money initially, you can diversify right away. Most individuals, however, start small and work toward their wealth goal. In the case of starting small, diversity can be managed through mutual funds and/or exchange traded funds (ETF's.) Exchange Traded Funds are traded like individual stocks in that they have real-time pricing, and you can buy and sell during the day. Earlier in this book we advised against mutual funds. Mutual funds can, however, be a practical option for modest starts. In this case, look carefully at the cost of the funds. Vanguard Funds are among the lowest cost funds available, and you can find a lot of Vanguard funds at a total cost of 0.2% per year. Mutual funds prices do not fluctuate during the day. These fund prices are typically established based on NAV (Net Asset Value) at the end of each trading day.

Both Mutual Funds and ETFs have a distinct advantage for the small investor; they offer diversification. Diversification can and should be established across market sectors, too. As an example, you could choose to invest in stocks of companies engaged in mining, energy, healthcare, biotech, and consumer goods.

Strategy #7:
Do not put an excessive percentage of your holdings into a single equity.

If you are starting with a modest amount, stay away from equities (stocks.) You should look at funds and ETF's. Once you get enough wealth to have 3-5 individual stock positions, try to have them approximately equally distributed. For instance, if you have 5 stocks, your target should be 20% of your investment dollars in each stock. If you can have a portfolio of 20 or more stocks, you can set a target of approximately 5%. It is ok to knowingly have more (say 7.5% or so) if you really like the stock but recognize that you are increasing the risk of loss if that specific stock has a downturn.

The prior history of the US Auto company stocks illustrates the risk clearly. They were riding high and company stock shares were provided to the employees as part of their investment plan. Some people had 100% of their investments in company stock. When these stocks fell from their soaring levels to virtually nothing in the 2007/2008 downturn, the value of all of the employees' career-long investments went to near zero. In fact, GM shares did go to zero in the restructuring. Ford went to a low of just over $1.00/share and appears to be making a slow comeback as of the time of this writing.

Rebalancing is a technique to avoid becoming too dependent on a single stock. Later, we will discuss how to review and rebalance your portfolio in a quarterly review.

Strategy #8:
Read a few good books about investing

My highest recommendation is The *Intelligent Investor,* revised edition by Benjamin Graham, with preface and appendix by Warren E. Buffett and updated with new commentary by Jason Zweig.

I would also recommend *Debunkery* by Ken Fisher. This book looks at the money-killing myths of Wall Street.

Finally, especially as a beginner, do not fall into some magic system of software for charting, timing, or any other substitute for doing your own research.

Choosing a Broker

I do not have extensive experience outside of Scottrade and Fidelity. Of these two, I prefer Scottrade because of comfort with the ease of access to stock research. Also, Scottrade has premium software, Scottrade Elite, which you can use if your account is over $25,000. It has real-time data for pricing as well as all of the fundamental measurements which you need to make decisions.

While I feel comfortable with Scottrade and their software, this is because I happen to use them for personal investments. Your choice of investment broker is a personal one and all of the major on-line brokers have very fine software packages.

Selecting Stocks

This section contains a brief outline of one method of selecting stocks. A detailed discussion on selecting stocks is in Appendix I.

The software from your on-line broker will include a "Stock Screener." There are additional stock screeners available on the internet. Both Google and Yahoo have basic stock screeners. See the links below:
https://www.google.com/finance/stockscreener, or
http://screener.finance.yahoo.com/stocks.html

A stock screener is possibly the single most valuable tool you can use. Some on-line brokers have a basic stock screener free on the internet. Once you establish an account, you have access to a far superior stock screener than what the broker offers to the public. For the purposes of the examples below, the Scottrade account stock screener was used.

There are many ways you can use the screener to drill down and find a selection of stocks to consider for investment. The following is an outline of one method that I use extensively.

The assumption is that we have a little more than $5000 to invest and we want to invest that in 100 shares of a single equity at approximately $50/share. Here are the steps to set up the screener:

STOCK SCREENER SETUP

Note: This data is based on January 13, 2013, Scottrade stock-screener output.

The following screener selections are made under the tab named "Price Performance"

1. Select: *share price $40-52/share.* (This resulted in 444 stocks within the $40-52/share

2. Select: *S&P Cap IQ STAR Ranking 4 and 5* (This further reduced the 444 stocks to a total of 54)

3. Select: Reuters Ratings *Positive* (This resulted in a total of 22 stocks (see symbols below) highly rated by both S&P and Reuters and also priced between $40-52/share)

> (AET, ATW, BLL, CBT, CAH, CBI, C, CVS, HAR, HEI, HFC, IACI, IR, JEC, JPM, MGA, MTX, NFG, PCAR, POT, STT, TJX)

At this point, you will get a spreadsheet with all 22 stocks listed above.

Next, go to the tab titled "Earnings and Dividends."

1. If you are interested in dividends, you can click the column titled "Dividend Yield" and order it so the highest dividend stocks are on top. This data resulted in the following stocks with greater than 2%

dividend yield (NFG @ 2.96%, JPM @ 2.62%, CAH at 2.55%, IACI at 2.21% and MGA at 2.14%.

Note that this group is already diversified among sectors:
NFG = Natural Gas Utilities
JPM = Money Center Banks
CAH = Biotechnology and Drugs
IACI = Computer Services
MGA = Auto and Truck Parts.

2. If you are not specifically interested in dividends, you may be interested in revenue growth during the Current Fiscal Year. You can similarly sort that column to show the top five stocks in this category. This data resulted in 3 stocks with greater than 20% revenue growth. (IACI @ 35.59%, ATW at 27.88%, and HFC at 25.30 %.)

In our simple analysis, IACI begins to look pretty good since it is one of the top stocks in both dividend yield and revenue growth.

The sector diversity in this group is as follows:
IACI = Computer Services
ATW = Oil Well Services & Equipment
HFC = Oil and Gas Operations

Now we have identified 7 stocks which are highly rated by two major rating agencies and they have a few areas in which they excel from similar stocks in their group, namely highest dividend yield (5) and highest revenue growth (3).

At this point, we have already done more than a lot of people when they select a stock. It is recommended that you do more, however, and that is discussed in Appendices I and II

In order to make the best buy, you need to pick top stocks and you have to know when to buy them. This is tricky and a few approaches are discussed in the section titled *"Making the Purchase."*

Making the Purchase

There are many factors which can impact the timing of a stock buy. These include, but are not limited to the following:

Current price vs. 52 week High and Low

Recent news about the specific stock

The latest upgrades or downgrades of the stock

The overall economy as it may apply to all stocks

The sector performance that the specific stock belongs to

The US vs. the World economy as it applies to the stock in question (i.e., is it a global stock?)

Geo-political concerns

Mega trends (example #1 - we are facing 18 years of baby boomers coming into retirement age – health care and drugs seem like they should be growth sectors. Example #2 – Natural gas is found in abundance in North America due to hydraulic fracturing. This will impact energy costs and attract high-energy consuming business to North America.)

Some stocks are cyclic.

New legislation may impact some stocks (i.e., biofuels, windfarms, and solar energy)

New technology - Internet business (i.e., printed books are threatened and it looks like internet purchases are going to greatly reduce Best Buy and other similar businesses)

There are ways you can place an order so that you lower the cost of the brokerage fees and also improve your chances of buying at an attractive price

1. Limit Option:

You can choose to make your purchase or sale using the "Limit" option. With this option, you state the price you are willing to either buy or sell. This is highly recommended. The common alternative is to use the "Market" price which would be whatever the Bid or Sell price is at the time you place your order. Note that there are two prices listed when a stock is trading. "Bid" is what price people are willing to pay for the stock. "Sell" is what people are willing to accept for the stock. The difference is called the "Spread." Most of the stocks you will deal with have a small spread, usually $0.01/share to $0.02/share. If you deal with low volume and/or low-priced stocks, the spread can be large and will be your loss when you finally sell.

2. AON Option:

If you buy or sell in blocks of 100 shares or more, you can use the "AON" option (All or None.) This means that you will avoid the unintended possibility of selling your 100 shares in smaller lots and multiplying your brokerage costs. As an example, purchasers could buy in 3 steps of, say, 50 shares, 30 shares and 20 shares. This would be 3 transactions and, assuming your brokerage fee is $7/transaction, it would cost you $21.00. (i.e., 3 x $7.00)

3. OCA Option:

There is a great option for a stock order which is listed as an "OCA" order. (One Cancels All.) With this option, you could select 3 stocks, all of which you would be happy to buy. You could then use this option to put in an order for each stock. The first order that sells will result in the cancellation of the other two orders. If you recall, earlier in our "Stock Screener" discussion we found 3 of the top dividend stocks:

NFG = Natural Gas Utilities
JPM = Money Center Banks
CAH = Biotechnology and Drugs

Using the OCA order, even though you are limited to $5000 total, you could place an order for all three of these stocks. To make sure you have a little advantage, you could place the order for 2% below the current market value for each of the above. When the first stock drops 2% from the current market value, you will own that stock and the other orders will be cancelled. This is a good option when you have no reason to expect that some major force is going to move the market either up or down.

At the time of this writing, we were looking at the fiscal cliff and at the debt ceiling. Both of these were (in my opinion) grandstanding acts by politicians which created fear in the public and garnered the politicians a little facetime with the press. These shenanigans create wild swings in the markets, but they have very little to do with the actual value of the individual companies you are trying to buy shares in. Even if the shares drop due to the panic, they will come back. This is to be differentiated from price drops due to bad economic news within a company or within the sector that it represents.)

If you have the time and you can watch the stocks at the time you expect them to trade, you can intervene to your advantage. As an example, if you had intended to buy at 2% below yesterday's market value, you may find the price dropping rapidly. At that point, you could drop the price considerably and watch for the point where the rapid fall levels off. It still may plateau and then drop further, but at least you did better than the original 2%. This technique could also result in your missing the purchase due to a sudden rise, but then you could go back to the 2% drop as per your initial order strategy.

Dividends

Cash dividends result in direct payment to the shareholder. In regular accounts, this becomes income and is taxed accordingly. In IRA accounts, this is treated the same as stock price appreciation and you will be taxed as ordinary income when you take distribution from your IRA.

It may be a great play to have dividends even if you pay taxes on them. If you had $500,000 in an account and it was making 4% dividends, you would enjoy $1667/month added to your income before taxes. If you do not need the dividend income, it most likely is best to buy stocks for value and growth and let the dividend income be of lesser importance. In any case, it is best to re-invest the dividends. You can do this by letting them accumulate in your account until they are significant and then make additional stock purchases with them. A few companies have "Stock Dividends." In this case, they provide added shares of stock instead of cash.

Selecting stocks strictly because of high dividends is a very risky business and a likely way to suffer a loss. There are published data for each company, and one very important and easy to find data point is something called "Payout Ratio." This is defined as (Dividends/share divided by Earnings/share). Typically, the Payout Ratios for healthy companies which pay dividends are 10% to 50% and perhaps even higher – maybe 75%. Some companies are near or even over 100%. When this happens, it is a disaster waiting to happen. There are two obvious possibilities: (1) they will lower or even cease their dividends, or (2) they will run out of money. Most companies with very high dividend payouts are in trouble and all you must do to find it is look at their fundamentals, especially their Payout Ratio. A final warning is that when a company drops its dividend, people get disappointed and sell. This drives the share price down causing further erosion of your portfolio value.

When you received dividends in an IRA, you do not have to pay taxes upon receipt. These dividends then can accumulate in your account until such time that you can make another purchase of your most favored stocks.

Quarterly Review

Once you have made your purchases and you have a growing portfolio, your ongoing work consists of managing additional purchases. These can be made if you make a sale or when your contributions and dividends accumulate.

The purpose of the quarterly review is to reaffirm that the stocks which looked so good to you still look good. Additionally, you want to determine if you need to rebalance your stocks.

I recommend creating an Excel spreadsheet which includes all of the fundamental values for each of your stocks. This is discussed in Appendix II.

Once you have your spreadsheet, rate all stocks as Green, Yellow, or Red. This rating is just a way to sort out the group to the best, the middle, and the worst of the group. It does not mean the worst rated ones are bad stocks. These are the ones you would sacrifice if you needed to for special reasons. These may be ones which have been recently downgraded by S&P or otherwise lost intrinsic value.

Do you need to rebalance?

In dollar terms does any single stock represent an inordinate % of value of the entire portfolio? (i.e. if the portfolio consists of 5 stocks and one stock represents 40% of the portfolio, one should consider selling back to the 20-25% level. Then the proceeds of the sale could be used to buy some highly rated under-represented stock or a new stock.

A thorough review of all your stocks is recommended at least twice/year. If time permits, quarterly would be preferable. This does not mean that you have to sell/buy to precisely rebalance, but you should have an awareness of any disproportionality within your portfolio. The dangers of being overweight in any stock are widely discussed. Many people held a monolithic block of stock from the company for which they worked. It can be felt that high holdings are a source of pride and show loyalty. When the going gets rough, the stock falls. Those that hold the stock are left holding the bag. If you diversify, you completely eliminate the possibility of a single stock from causing your financial ruin. Since some (most) high quality stocks are expected to rise over the long term, any stock that underperforms will have a small effect on your total portfolio.

Performance over time

Highly rated stocks, as a group, rise significantly over time. There are spectacular exceptions on the negative side, of course. Examples in the 2007/08 era include almost every stock listed. It is interesting to note, however, that the highly rated stocks which did fall during 2007/08 recovered at least by 2009/10. Not only did they recover but they generally came back to the same growth line that would have been predicted before the 07/08 recession. A very good example of this fact would be seen by looking at a 20-year chart of General Mills (GIS.)

Currently, my personal portfolio was just rebalanced. This effort took about 8 hours to complete. I ended up selling a large amount of CMI because it was far more than the 5% maximum, I feel comfortable with. I still think CMI is a great stock, but there are others. I bought several biotech stocks with the proceeds of the CMI sale: CELG, GILD, ALXN, and AGN.

Within my prior portfolio, the top "Green" stocks (i.e., the most highly rated by my system) were evaluated for total gain since January 4th, 2005. These ranged from 74% gain to 443% gain. The 443% gain was an exception (CMI), but the others were ABT @ 74% gain, GIS at 102% gain, IBM at 124% gain and KO at 128% gain. There were some spectacular gains in the middle "Yellow" stocks;

however, there was more variability within the "Yellow" group. This group ranged from -91% (C) yes, that is a minus, to 543% (ARMH). The average 7-year performance for all stocks in the portfolio was 131%. This is a deceptive number because it included the 2007/08 recession. An analysis of the same stocks over 2009-present would look considerably better.

On the next page you can see a table with 9 stocks shown. This list of stocks was developed using a stock screener with a simple sort. The sort criteria were S&P ratings, Reuters ratings, Current year EPS growth, and Current year Revenue growth. The right-hand column shows the appreciation of the stock from 2010 through January 16, 2013. As you can see, the average of the 9 stocks was 65.3% which outperformed the DJI at a 3-year gain of 27.7%.

These stocks were picked because they excelled among other very good stocks. In this instance, even the lowest performing stock (GIS at 27.4%) was performing equally to the DJI at 27.7%, whereas the best performer (CMI at 149%) had an appreciation more than 5 times the DJI.

Total gain of highly rated stocks selected using Scottrade Stock Screener		
S&P stars	Symbol	Adjusted Gain (1) 1/1/10 to 1/16/13
4	MCD	59.32%
4	GIS	27.43%
5	CVX	59.44%
3	ORCL	43.50%
4	IBM	53.23%
5	CMI	148.97%
3	GPC	89.97%
5	KO	42.77%
5	CVS	63.23%
	Average	**65.32%**
	Notes:	
	(1) Adjusted for splits and dividends	
	Note: DJI total gain for the same period was 27.66%	
	Caution: This analysis looks back in time.	

Table illustrating Chapter 7 – How have highly rated stocks performed over time

Alternative investments

This book is intended to focus on helping people who have already decided that they would like to buy stocks and/or ETFs.

Everyone knows there are no guarantees. Even if you save your money as cash, you lose because inflation eats away at your buying power. If Certificate of Deposit (CD) rates ever improve, CDs may be a safer alternative to equities. Bonds and bond funds have their own risk. One place that you could put money is an investment grade corporate bond fund. LQD is one of the largest ETFs in investment grade corporate bonds. There are others. These have had a history of a nice dividend (about 4 to 5% paid monthly) and they tend to be stable or improve. You may want to investigate such a fund if you feel stocks are not for you.

There are many other investment opportunities which are used successfully to build wealth. These alternate investments are not within the scope of this book. If you are drawn to any investment, be sure to do what you can to understand its risks and rewards.

Appendix I

Research – How to research a stock and build a "buy" List

The easiest way to research a stock is to use research which is provided to you as a rating service from your on-line broker. Scottrade provides the Standard and Poors (S&P) star rating (Now renamed CFRA) on most of the stocks. If you start with a list of 4-star and 5-star stocks, you are off to a good start. In fact, you are far better than building your list by listening to friends or talking heads. If you choose this method of building your buy list, you are also encouraged to do some additional research work, namely, glance at the firm's **SUMMARY, FUNDAMENTALS, EARNINGS, and FINANCIAL STATEMENTS.** These bold font topics are usually tabs or links within the broker's on-line software. Each of the above will be discussed below with selected metrics which are relevant to evaluating a potential investment.

SUMMARY
This summary has been prepared using CVS Caremark Corp (CVS) data of 1/24/13

> *S&P Cap IQ Ranking (*****), or 5-stars; the highest rating from Standard & Poors.*

> *Current share price, (52.46)*

52 week High/Low range relative to current price, (52.73/41.48)

Market Capitalization, (65.4B)

Shares outstanding, (1.2B)

EPS, earnings per share, TTM, Twelve Trailing Months, (2.98)

P/E Ratio, (17.6x)

Dividend Yield, (1.71%)

Ex-Date, (1/22/2013) (This is the date that current stockholders of record will be paid the next dividend)

Payable, (0.225 per QRTR).

FUNDAMENTALS – There is a wealth of information under the category of "Fundamentals." The following discussion describes the stock fundamentals. This data is very important for evaluating the list of stocks which already carry a high rating by S&P or other ratings firms.

Profitability, *including Gross Margin (18.13%), Operating Margin (5.73%) Pretax Margin (5.28%) and Net Profit Margin (3.21%)*

Negative numbers are generally a signal to avoid that stock unless there is a short-term factor which is explained. Very small positive numbers are obviously red flags, too. In the case of CVS, the numbers are a little low, but not especially distressing.

Financial Strength

Current Ratio (MRQ), Most Recent Quarter, (1.4) This is the product of Current Assets divided by Current Liabilities.

Quick Ratio (MRQ) (0.6) This is similar to the Current Ratio, but it subtracts inventories from current assets.

Note that the difference between Current Ratio and Quick ratio (0.8) is an expression of the size of the inventory held by the company. Smaller inventories are better.

Growth. Again, avoid stocks with negative numbers.

Sales (5Yr) (19.57%)

EPS, TTM over TTM (18.82%)

Dividend Growth, 5Yr (26.39%)

When you are comparing two equities that are otherwise very desirable, you may want to favor the one with the best growth numbers.

Per Share Data

BV/Share (MRQ), (29.63)

Tangible BV per share (MRQ), (0.56)

Cash per share (TTM), (0.99)

CVS has a book value of $35.6B. This is derived from 1.2B shares and a BV/Share of $29.63. A general rule is that the book value should be at least 50% of the capitalized value. In this case, we have (35.6)/65.4) = 54.4%. Therefore, CVS Caremark meets this test. This rule is not absolute, but you should be aware of it and certainly be wary of firms which have major violations of this rule. (Note: The rule for utilities is "at least 30 %.")

The Tangible Book Value typically is equal to, or very close to the book value. The difference is that Book Value also contains intangible assets, primarily Brand name, Patents, Good Will, etc. In this case, CVS has a large book value per share, but a tiny Tangible book value per share. This highlights a weakness in the CVS fundamentals. Note that Tangible Book Value is the actual value that the assets of the company could be sold for. One useful distinction between "book value" and "tangible book value" is that the assets in the book value are physical entities that can actually be touched.

The cash per share (MRQ), (0.99) can be used to calculate total cash held by CVS. Since CVS has 1.2B shares and $0.99 cash/share, it has $1.18B in total cash.

Short Ratio (1.7)

This is worth a glance. The higher this number is, the more that investors feel that the share price will drop. In the case of CVS, only 1.7% of the current traders are selling the stock short. This is a very low number, and it suggests that most traders do not think the stock will drop. Typically, we see short ratios in the range of 5 to 10. You should become cautious when you see short ratios significantly above 10.

EARNINGS

Many sources, including Scottrade, publish graphic output of various data for each equity. In the case of CVS, you can see that the EPS (earnings per share) appear to be cyclic. They rise for 4 quarters and then begin a new cycle. We would have to investigate longer periods to see if the cyclic trend holds true on a regular basis.

The chart below indicates that CVS met the expectations of the analysts which cover this equity. In cases where the stock falls short or exceeds the analysts' expectations, the individual bars will be coded with a minus (-) or plus (+) and the specific size of the variance from expectations.

CVS Quarterly Earnings Graph

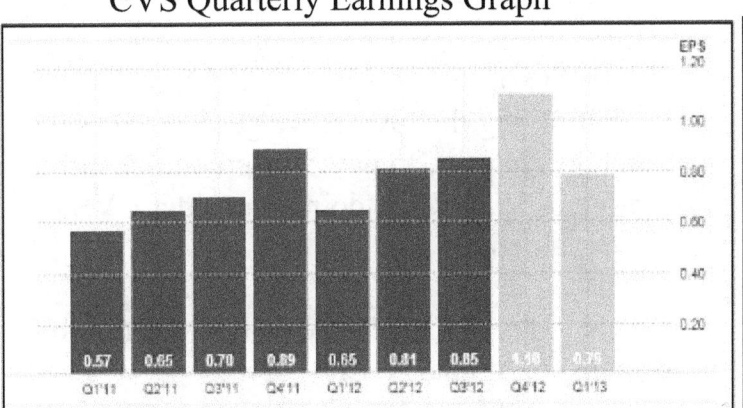

FINANCIAL STATEMENTS

The table below is the top line and the bottom line of the CVS Income Statement. Two basic observations can be made: (1) Their Total Revenue has raised from $76,078 to $107,100 in the 5 years 2007 to 2011. There was a dip in the 2010 Total Revenue, but it apparently recovered in 2011.

The Diluted Normalized EPS similarly increased from $1.92 to $2.59 at the same timeframe and it also showed evidence of the dip in 2010.

A recommended calculation (Benjamin Graham) is to look at the average EPS for a 7-year period. Graham suggests that the maximum price to pay is 25 times the average EPS. In this case, we will use 5 years. The Average of the 5 years EPS is $2.364. Multiplying that by 25, we get $59.10 as the maximum price to pay. Based on the current price of $52.17, we do not consider CVS to be overvalued.

This looks like a healthy company from this snapshot of data.

INCOME

CVS Income Statement

12 Month Period Ending Currency & US Dollar	12/31/2011 52 Weeks	12/31/2010 52 Weeks Restated 12/31/2011	12/31/2009 52 Weeks Restated 12/31/2011	12/31/2008 52 Weeks Restated 12/31/2011	12/29/2007 52 Weeks Reclassified 12/31/2011
Total revenue	107,100	96,778	98,215	87,005	76,078
Diluted Normalized EPS	2.59	2.49	2.55	2.27	1.92

The above table shows a *yearly* CVS income statement. You can also get the same data set but based on five *quarterly* income statements. The quarterly data is also worth a glance at the top and bottom lines to see which way the revenue and EPS values are trending over the short term.

Appendix II

Periodic Review of Stocks

	A	B	C	D	E	F	G	H	I	J	K	L	M
1	Results of Stock Sorter Exercise based on 1/24/13 data. Note that the table below is folded into two sections												
2	Symbol	Share Price	Dv%	52H	52L	Cur. price as % below 52H	Date of 5* S&P	Reuters Rating	Cap Val $B	P/E	Shares out, M	Trend	LT Debt
3	AAPL	520.91	1.99	7.05	3.4	54.18%	11/14/2012	P8	497.5	12	940.7	dwn last 2 qtr	0
4	BBT	26.62	27	34.37	23.45	43.60%	12/10/2012	N7	20.7	11.6	699.6	up	0.9
5	BIDU	100.96	100.66	0	154.15	76.16	4/25/2012	N6	35.2	22.6	349.3	up beat expect	0
6	CBOE	29.61	1.99	30.96	24.44	20.58%	9/24/2012	P8	2.6	17.7	87.3	flat bear ex	0
7	CIS	50.27	1.49	53.4	34.51	16.57%	8/11/2011	P8	88.1	16.1	1800	flat bear ex	0.3
8	ESS	144.95	3.04	161.53	136.87	64.61%	1/13/2012	N5	5.3	66.4	30.5	up beat expect	1.6
9	QCOM	62.915	1.56	69.67	61.76	36.39%	4/26/2012	P9	107	20.6	1700	flat bear ex	0
10	RJF	39.52	1.42	39.98	28.86	4.22%	7/9/2012	P8	5.5	17.8	138.4	up	0.4

			Payout Ratio	Sales Growth 5 yr, %	EPS Growth TTM %	Div growth 5 yr, %	Tangible BV/S	Cash/ share	Short Ratio	Total Cash $M	% of share (Cash + TBV)	EPS Growth Cur Fiscal Yr	Rev Growth Cur Fiscal Yr
11	Symbol	Total Debt											
12	AAPL	0	6	44.8	59.9		120.2	31.1	1	29171.1	28.60%	11.57%	22.98%
13	BBT	1.1	29.6	-0.02	82.04	-16.49	17.84	2.23	2.5	1560.11	67.80%	48.45%	11.08%
14	BIDU	C.1		0	76.87	88.90	0	9.12	9.77	1.8	3412.66	18.70%	57.28%	53.08%
15	CBOE	0	30.9	14.94	12.99		2.57	1.84	5.5	150.632	15.20%	3.50%	-0.31%
16	CIS	C.4	18.9	3.65	24.17	11.38	2.83	1.88	6	3084	9.40%	11.40%	6.20%
17	ESS	1.6	204	7.3	177	4.3	46.76	0.75	5.4	27375	32.60%	123.30%	12.74%
18	QCOM	0	30.2	16.6	13.11	12.59	16.65	7.25	1.7	12325	38.40%	18.17%	23.38%
19	RJF	C.5	24.1	4.62	310	5.39	21.11	14.3	3	1983.27	89.70%	21.51%	16.49%

The above chart is busy, and it is not expected that anyone will study it carefully. It is presented just for its overall layout of a recommended tool for reviewing stocks. This example shows stocks selected using the stock screener, but the same exercise can be used with the stocks in a personal account. Below is a discussion what this chart tells us along with what the individual columns mean.

To make this chart, 70 stocks were selected that were 5-Star rated by S&P. Data was then entered in the columns directly from the Scottrade "Quotes & Research" page. Appendix III contains an explanation of each column. For those who may not be familiar with spreadsheets, Columns are vertical displays of data and Rows are horizontal displays of data. All data for a single company will be displayed on a single row. When you view a single column, you can compare all the companies on the list for a given fundamental such as *Percent Dividend.*

Once the data is loaded, the sorting feature of the spreadsheet can be used to sort one column at a time. As an example, you could sort on column C, dividend percent. Cells within the column can be highlighted after the sort. Green highlighting indicates those cells at the top (best) of that column, while red highlighting is used to indicate the lowest within the chosen stocks. The stocks which are in the middle (not top or bottom) are shaded yellow.

Thus, we would shade ESS (3.04%) and BBT (2.7%) green as the top dividend payers, and BIDU (0%) would be shaded red as the lowest. We would then perform a similar sort and shading on all columns that had values that could be judged relative to each other.

When we are done with exercise, we have a visual color chart which helps us to make the purchase decision of one stock over the other. In this case, the more green shading on a given row, the better that stock is relative to the others.

Note: High dividends may be good if you are looking for dividends for income, but based on your particular situation, you may not want dividends due to the tax impact or other considerations. Also, beware of very high dividends. You can check to see if they are sustainable by looking at the Payout Ratio. If the Payout Ratio is over 60%, it should throw up a red flag. If it is over 100%, the dividend probably cannot be maintained.

Appendix III

Explanation of spreadsheet columns in Appendix II

Description of Columns

A. The stock symbols

B. The current share price of the stock on that row

C. The current percent dividend the stock is yielding.

D. The 52-week *high* share price

E. The 52-week *low* share price

F. This is the current share price expressed as a percent below the 52-week high price.

G. The date on which the current S&P 5-star rating was made.

H. The Reuter's rating. Neutral or Positive and 0-10 rated.

I. The Capitalized Value of the stock in $Billions.

J. The P/E (price to earnings) ratio

K. The number of shares outstanding, millions.

L. Observational data based on reviewing the earnings by quarter.

M. Long Term Debt to Equity ratio

N. Total Debt to Equity Ratio

O. Payout ratio

P. Five-year sales growth, %

Q. EPS growth, %, TTM (Twelve Trailing Months)

R. Five-year Dividend growth, %

S. Tangible Book Value per share

T. Cash per share

U. Short Ratio

V. Total Cash

W. Cash plus Tangible Book Value expressed as a percent of the share price.

X. EPS growth during the current fiscal year

Y. Revenue growth during the current fiscal year

Appendix IV

Selected Definitions:

Cash Flow/share
((Operating Cash Flow) - (Preferred Dividends)) / (Common Shares Outstanding)

Current Ratio
(Current Assets) / Current Liabilities

Gross Margin
((Revenue) - (Cost of Goods Sold)) / (Net Sales)

LT Debt/Equity
(Total Liability) / (Shareholders equity)

Net Margin
(Net Profit) / (revenue)

Net Profit
(Revenue) - (Cost of Goods Sold) - (Operating Expense) - (Interest & taxes)

Op Margin
(Operating Income) / (Net Sales)

Options Expire
3rd Fri - see also Triple witching

Overbought
Price at levels that do not support the fundamentals (Stochastics)

Oversold
Price at levels below its true value (Stochastics)

Payout Ratio
(Dividend/share) / (Earnings per share)

PE Ratio
[(Share Price) / (Earnings (Profit)], or (Price) / (EPS)

PEG Ratio
(Price/Earnings Ratio) / Annual EPS growth
{0=PE<Growth, 2=PE>growth}

Price/Sales Ratio
(Price) / (Revenue/share) TTM The lower the better
(i.e.: is a stock cheap?)

Quick Ratio
(Current Assets - Inventories) / Current Liabilities

Return on Assets
(Net Income) / (Total Assets)

Return on Equity
(Net Income) / (Shareholder's Equity)

Return on Investments
((Gain on Investments) - (Cost of Investments)) / Cost of investments

Shareholder Equity
(Total Assets) - (Total Liability)

Short Interest
Number of shares sold short

Short Ratio
Shares Sold Short) / (Average daily trading volume)

Short Ratio (Technical Investor Confidence)
(# shares sold short) / Avg daily trading volume
{>5.0 = bullish, <3.0 = bearish}"

Tangible BV/Share
(Total tangible assets (aka BV)) / (No. of shares outstanding)

Total Equity
(Total assets) minus (Total liabilities) This is a key metric to watch over time for growth.

Triple Witching

3rd Fri of Mar/Jun/Sep/Dec. This is an event that impacts stock prices and results from the simultaneous expiration of contracts for stock index futures, stock index options, and stock options.

A few useful Formulas for evaluating stocks:

Max price

Max price to pay = (25) X (Average 7-year EPS)

Book Value limit

BV should be at least 50% of total capitalized value (30% for utilities) (Comment – This is outdated and very few companies meet this criterion. Generally though, the higher the better)

BV/Share

((Total Shareholders' equity) - (Preferred Equity)) / (Total Outstanding Shares)

The above formulae are suggested in Benjamin Graham's book, "The Intelligent Investor."

Appendix V

Author's notes:

Early in this book there was a cautionary note against speculation. If you still have an appetite for this type of "action," the suggestion is offered that you have a small budget for this purpose and have fun. Do not plan to make money at this game. If you do, realize that it is somewhat like getting all "sevens" on a slot machine. You can tip the odds a little by using a stock selector and finding penny stocks (Generally low-priced stocks under $5.00) that have no debt and some positive trends.

In the discussion of evaluating stocks, it may seem like an impossible task when you start. You can be assured that once you assess five or six companies, you will be more comfortable with the process, and you will find the level of research suggested to be fast and easy. Also, once you have a little experience in this area, you may customize your assessment to fit your needs.

Brace yourself to avoid panic when the economy takes a dip. If an overall force such as government dysfunctionality (i.e., Debt Ceiling, Budget Approval, etc) puts fear in the market and your stocks go down, this has nothing to do with the valuation and potential growth of your stocks. It is generally bad to sell in such a situation. In fact, this would be a good time to buy because the stocks you hold are depressed for reasons not relating to the stock itself.

To greatly simplify the overall stock market, it can be viewed as similar to sitting in a cabana at the ocean beach and watching the water lapping against the sand.

There are periodic waves which have a repeat up and down motion. This is like daily trading fluctuations.

There are big events (tides) which cause the level to rise or fall for significant periods of time. This is like overall market fear because of major news which is not directly related to the stocks. (i.e., Terrorist event, government dysfunction, etc)

There is a third event where both the periodic waves and the tides have a constant overall direction. An example of this would be rising sea levels due to global warming. In this analogy, it is like the changing stock share prices of individual companies. Well managed companies' share prices may rise and fall just like the periodic waves, but over the long term they go up more than they fall, and we have share price growth.

There is another factor that doesn't have an analogy in this simplified "ocean beach" view. This is when an individual company has some major event which is based on the company's management effectiveness or other-directed actions. It could be the announcement of a significantly better financial report than was expected. It could be a breakthrough product which has the potential for billions of dollars of new revenue. On the downside, there are many similar examples such as a federal investigation into business practices, news reports of a fabled CEO leaving, etc.

The internet is full of wonderful investing resources. Yahoo Finance and Google Finance are tops. Another great source is Nasdaq. With the Nasdaq website, you can get a quick look at what the analysts are saying about any stock. Also, they have a feature named "Guru Analysis." In this feature, there are blue circular targets which are shaded yellow in accordance with each Guru's rating of 0-100. You will find some Gurus are wild about a stock while others want nothing to do with it. This is because some are looking for value and/or growth while others are looking for other indicators. If you click on the yellow and blue target, you can delve into the formulae used to make the assessment and see exactly what indicator caused a particular Guru to develop his/her assessment.

http://finance.yahoo.com
http://www.google.com/finance
http://www.nasdaq.com
http://www.nasdaq.com/quotes/stock-guru-analysis.aspx

Bottom line: Establish a conservative long term investment plan. Buy highly rated stocks with good fundamentals. Take control of your own investments and watch it grow. Review your portfolio at least twice a year and balance it as necessary. Do not succumb to using this money for special expenses. The longer your time horizon, the bigger will be your reward.

This book was originally published in 2013 and while some references are outdated, the principles are solid. There were a few updates made to make the message meaningful in terms of the 2022 markets.

I hope you will find this book helpful. If you have recommendations for corrections or otherwise to improve it, please let me know.
mcpozz@gmail.com

Acknowledgements:

Thank you to those of you who have read the draft of this book and recommended corrections and improvements.

Madelon Possley
Russell Possley
Murray Meisels
Jeff Smith
Rob Malan

www.ingramcontent.com/pod-product-compliance
Lightning Source LLC
Chambersburg PA
CBHW071648170526
45166CB00003B/1479